D1572735

MOOSE MOMENTS

CONSONANT DIGRAPHS

by Jacqueline Vinesse

Illustrated by Elizabeth Taylor

MOOSE MOMENTS: CONSONANT DIGRAPHS

Written by Jacqueline Vinesse

Illustrated by Elizabeth Taylor

Edited by Charles Taylor, Janet Jones, Terri Tamres

Cover Image: Elizabeth Taylor

Layout: Elizabeth Taylor, Janet Jones, Dan Mackey

© 2011 Moose Materials
ISBN-13: 978-1463501433
ISBN-10: 1463501439

ABOUT MOOSE MOMENTS

The aim of Moose Moments is to provide the teacher or parent with a resource for the reinforcement of the various phonograms, syllable types, and spelling rules encountered by the student who is learning to read and write.

A major influence behind this series of books is the organizational system of the Orton-Gillingham approach. This approach has been designed to increase reading success in the struggling reader, notably by arranging the structure of the English language into a sequence of increasing complexity which is then systematically taught. While this series can be used to provide practice for the struggling reader, it is not limited to the student who is experiencing difficulties. Instead, we feel that anyone faced with the task of grasping the complexities of English could benefit from this collection of stories and poems.

Each book consists of a number of stories and poems that have been written to exemplify a particular phonogram, syllable type, or spelling rule. To facilitate instruction, a definition of the concept targeted by each book is provided adjacent to the table of contents. In addition, each story is followed by a list of words that may not be recognized by the student, either because they typically occur later in the sequence, or because they are irregular words. (If required, these words can be given directly to the student.) We have also included a small number of definitions, essentially to serve as a quick reference for the teacher or parent.

There are a number of ways in which Moose Moments can be used: as practice reading material, as generators of word lists pertaining to a particular concept, or as a means to explore other areas underpinning linguistic competence such as rhyme, rhythm, and word play. In our view, however, one of the most important ways this collection can be used is in promoting the idea that reading can be fun!

TARGETED CONCEPT
CONSONANT DIGRAPHS

<u>Target Concept Definition</u>: Consonant Digraphs are two letters that represent one sound.   For example: th =/th/as in thumb, sh =/sh/as in ship, ch =/ch/as in chin, wh =/wh/as in whistle

The following high frequency words appear repeatedly in these stories, allowing readers to have extensive practice with the words: *he, she, we, be, to, too, there, said, have, what, there, they.* There are also a number of words that contain the beginning vowel teams "ee" and "oo", and a few which use "i-e" as in a silent-e syllable.

Note: This book contains a challenge section featuring a story and a poem that use more complex constructions and vocabulary than in the regular stories.   Words to Know lists have not been provided for the challenge section.

TABLE OF CONTENTS

CHALLENGE SECTION:

THE THIN MOTH

A thin moth went to have a bath, but his bathtub was filthy.
So the thin moth rubbed the bathtub with a cloth to get froth.

The thin moth's bathtub was still filthy. So the thin moth
had to think. Then he went on the path to see his pal, Bill Smith.
When he got there, Bill Smith handed him a cloth. Bill said to the
thin moth, "Have this cloth. It will be better than that cloth."

So the thin moth thanked his pal Bill Smith and went back on the path to his bathtub. He rubbed the bathtub with Bill's cloth until he had lots of froth.

Then his bathtub was not filthy. So the thin moth had a long bath. In fact, he was so thrilled with his bathtub that he had three baths! After his baths, the thin moth went on the path to give the cloth back to Bill Smith.

To thank Bill Smith, the thin moth fixed Bill and his mother a big pot of broth. That thrilled Bill Smith and his mother. It was the best broth ever!

THE THIN MOTH

WORDS TO KNOW

<u>High Frequency Decodable Words</u>

so, be, see, three

<u>High Frequency Irregular Words</u>

to, have, said, give, one, there, mother

<u>Definitions</u>

filthy – *very dirty*

broth – *soup*

BETH'S BATH

Beth was a tot. She liked lots of things. She liked to be with Mother and Father. She liked the dog and the cat. She liked to be in the grass and in the mud. But Beth did not like the bath.

In the bathtub, she sobbed, yelled, and splashed. Father asked, "Can we stop the bath until she likes it?" Mother said. "No, I do not think so. A tot has to have a bath."

The next day, Beth went with Mother to visit Mrs. Roth. She had just had a baby. His name was Seth and Beth liked him a lot.

Then Mrs. Roth said that Seth had to have a bath. "Can you help me?" she asked Beth. Beth looked at Mother. "Go on, Beth," said Mother, "You can be a big help."

So Beth went with Mrs. Roth and Seth. She sat next to the baby bathtub to see Seth in his bath. "See, Beth," said Mrs. Roth, "Seth likes his bath a lot."

What do you think happened when Beth had her next bath? She did not sob or splash. In fact, she liked the bath so much she did not want to get out!

BETH'S BATH

WORDS TO KNOW

High Frequency Decodable Words

be, we, she, me, no, so, go, see, name, liked, mother, father, baby, looked, or, her, want, out

High Frequency Irregular Words

of, to, you, said, have, what

THE FISH AND CHIP SHOP

Miss Trish had a wish. Her wish was to have a fish and chip shop, just like in England. What is a fish and chip shop? A fish and chip shop sells fresh, hot fish with hot chips.* Children in England like fish and chips a lot.

So Miss Trish kept her cash until she had a shop. She cooked lots of hot fish and hot chips, but no one stopped at the shop. Miss Trish was sad. "Oh, gosh," she said, "if I cannot sell the fish and chips, I will have to shut the shop."

Just then, Miss Trish's chum stopped at the shop. She was shocked that Miss Trish was so sad. "Why not pass out the fish and chips?" she said. So Miss Trish did just that. She went with a big dish of fresh fish and chips and handed them all out. Even children helped finish up the fish.

Now Miss Trish sells lots and lots of fish and chips. When the fish is all finished, she shuts up the shop. Then Miss Trish and her chum sit and chat -- with a big dish of fish and chips!

Footnote: In England, children call French fries "chips".

FISH AND CHIP SHOP
WORDS TO KNOW

<u>High Frequency Decodable Words</u>

her, England, children, like, so, she, why, out, all, even, now

<u>High Frequency Irregular Words</u>

to, have, what, one, said, one

<u>Definitions</u>

England – *a country that is part of Great Britain*

THE CHUMS AND THE CHIMP

It was Halloween, when lots of children go to "Boo in the Zoo." Chuck was going as a chicken. Chet was Chuck's best chum, and he was going as a chimp. He had on a chimp mask and in his hand, he held a bunch of bananas.

The chums went off to the zoo with the moms. At the zoo, lots of children were all dressed up. The staff was handing out lots of candy to the children.

When the bags had gotten filled to the top, Chuck and Chet sat on a bench. They munched on candy, and the moms had a chat. Just then there was a big yell. One of the chimps was not in his pen! The staff was hunting the zoo for the chimp.

As Chuck and Chet sat on the bench, there was a crunching up in the trees. "Look!" said Chuck. "It's the chimp!" As Chet's

mom ran off to get help, Chuck and Chet looked up at the chimp. It was sitting on a branch in a tree. The chimp was small and sad. "Chet!" said Chuck. "Get the bunch of bananas! See if the chimp will come."

So Chet held the bunch of bananas up to the chimp. "Come and get a banana, chimp," he said. "Look, I'm a chimp too." To help the chimp, Chet put his mask back on. The chimp got out of the tree and took a banana from Chet. Then Chuck fed him a banana too. The chimp sat on the bench with the chums and chomped on the bananas.

Then Chet's mom got back with the staff. She said, "The staff will help the chimp get back to his pen and his mom." To thank the chums, the staff handed them chicken nuggets and a big bag of chips. But for Chuck and Chet, the best thing was that the chimp got to check out "Boo in the Zoo."

THE CHUMS AND THE CHIMP
WORDS TO KNOW

High Frequency Decodable Words

he, so, going, for, see, trees, boo, zoo, too, look, all, out, candy, children, Halloween

High Frequency Irregular Words

to, put, said, come, they, there, bananas

Definitions

Boo in the Zoo: *Some zoos have parties on Halloween where children can visit the zoo all dressed up and get their bags filled with treats.*

CHALLENGE SECTION:

SAVE THE WHALE

To a ship with a wheel

That helped it to steer

There came up in a flash

A whale that went crash.

So the men on the ship

Ran to get a big whip

So the wheel they could lash

And the ship would not crash.

But the tail of the whale

Went swish, whish, and smash

So the ship lost its wheel

And could no longer steer.

So the men of the ship

Made a dash for the skiff

That would whisk them to shore

Ere their ship was no more.

But the whale was still there

Going Whee! Whoop! and Wham!

So they sent up a flare

So the whale would be scared.

Then the whale he did splash them

But he did not thrash them

And with a whisk and a frisk

He was gone.

So the men of the ship

Took off in the skiff

And made it to shore

As the ship was no more.

And still then to this day

They do talk of the way

They got whipped by a whale

But why?

Nobody knows

That's how it goes

Whoever can say

For sure?

Perhaps the whale with the tail

Had a wish or a whim

To make the men of the ship

Take a swim.

Then that way he'd know

That man was no foe

After

All.

For if the men of the boat

Had to stay up afloat

Then for sure

Man's a mammal

Like him!

THE H BROTHER CLOWNS

Once there were three brothers who were also clowns. Their names were Chubby, Shaggy and Whoopy. The circus called them The H Brother Clowns.

Chubby was the cheerful clown. Chubby liked food a lot. Every day he munched on chips, chops, chicken, chestnuts, and cheese. All the children who came to the circus cheered for Chubby because he was cheery, cheeky, and chubby.

Shaggy was the short clown. He had a hat with a fish on it and a shirt made of sea shells. He liked to splash people with water. All the children who came to the circus shouted for Shaggy because he looked silly and did silly things.

Whoopy was the whimsical clown. Whoopy liked to whoop and whistle a lot. When he was in the ring, Whoopy would twirl and whirl about. All the children who came to the circus whooped for Whoopy because he did lots of odd, whimsical things.

One very hot day, after church, Chubby, Shaggy and Whoopy wanted to have lunch at the beach. Chubby put chicken, chips, and cheese in a ice chest. Shaggy washed the car, and Whoopy put a white ball into the trunk.

The three chums rushed into the car. Whoopy took the wheel. Chubby sat beside the ice chest and chewed gum, while Shaggy shot peas from his pea-shooter. The three clowns were very happy to be on a trip.

When they got to the shore, Whoopy began to whoop. "I can see the sea! I can see ships!" he shouted. The three clowns put out their food onto a sheet on the grass then dashed onto the sand.

The clowns splashed in the water and played with the white ball. After a while, they began to get hungry and thirsty. They went back to the grass to have their lunch, but when they got there, they saw that the gulls had eaten all the food. Nothing was left on the sheet, only some chicken bones.

The three clowns were crushed. Now their day at the beach had gone bad. Chubby began to punch on a bench, Whoopy began to whisper sadly, and Shaggy began to wish they had never come. Just then, a class of children who were on a trip to the beach came up to the clowns. "You are The H Brother clowns," said the teacher. "Why are you so sad?"

"The gulls ate our food," sniffed Chubby. "Cheer up!" said the children. "You can share our food." So the class of children shared their food with the three clowns. Chubby became cheerful again, Whoopy began to whistle again, while Shaggy washed up all of the dishes.

To thank the children, the clowns did a show for the class on the sand. The children all shouted and cheered. When they had finished, the three clowns picked up lots of shells then took home a big dish of fish and shrimp for dinner.

JACQUELINE VINESSE

Jacqueline Vinesse holds a degree in Developmental Psychology from the University of Edinburgh and is an Orton-Gillingham trained tutor. Besides teaching psychology in Japan and South Carolina, she has spent a number of years working as a tutor and primary teacher at Camperdown Academy, Greenville, SC. She has two daughters and currently resides in France with her husband.

ELIZABETH TAYLOR

Most of her childhood years were spent in San Juan, Puerto Rico. As a child, she loved to imagine and draw--none of that has changed over the years. She never thought it would be much fun to be a "grown up", and in illustrating children's books she is able to stay young at heart. She has spent much of her life raising her own four children and teaching in elementary school.

Made in the USA
San Bernardino, CA
26 March 2016